WILTSHIRE RAMBLES

ROGER JONES

With Historical Notes

COUNTRYSIDE BOOKS
NEWBURY, BERKSHIRE

First Published 1983
Revised Edition 1985
Reprinted 1987
New Revised edition 1989
© Roger Jones 1983, 1985, 1987 and 1989

COUNTRYSIDE BOOKS
3 Catherine Road
Newbury, Berkshire
ISBN 0 905392 50 7

Books by Roger Jones
published by Ex Libris Press:
A Book of Newton Abbot
Where Wiltshire meets Somerset
Down the Bristol Avon
Green Road to Land's End
Betwixt Moor and Sea

Edited and Introduced by Roger Jones:
The Walker's Companion
West Country Tour

Cover photograph reproduced by courtesy of
the West Country Tourist Board

Printed by J. W. Arrowsmith Ltd., Bristol

Contents

WILTSHIRE RAMBLES

Introduction

Wiltshire is chalk and cheese: the chalk uplands cover more than half the county and provide a sweeping downland landscape of singular beauty. It is an open country characterised by crops growing in large fields, sheep grazing on slopes too steep for cultivation; all spread out beneath huge skies. As if to emphasise the spaciousness of the scene clumps of trees, usually beech, cling to patches of clay on the chalk ridges like ships on a great rolling sea. The chalk downs are intersected by wide valleys whose rivers are fed by springs flowing from the base of the porous chalk strata.

The second element of the chalk and cheese comprises the clay vales of north and west Wiltshire whose heavy soils are best suited to dairying. Here are fields and meadows providing rich pasture for cattle. In addition, the north western corner of the county constitutes the eastern and southern edge of the Cotswolds whose distinctive creamy stone is so evident in the buildings of its towns and villages.

Wiltshire's industries have traditionally been associated with the produce of the land. Apart from agriculture and food processing, most notable among these was the wool and cloth industry which now, with the exception of the famous carpet factory at Wilton, is all but extinct, though much remains to remind one of its former importance.

Wiltshire is unusually rich in well preserved manor houses and there are some splendid examples of all periods from the medieval to the Victorian. Add to these the precious parish churches, the unspoilt villages and the small country towns, each with its own distinctive flavour, and we have a county with much to offer the curious rambler.

In addition to its roads, canals and railways (many of which are now disused), Wiltshire possesses some 2,500 miles of public footpaths. One of Britain's most famous long distance paths, the Ridgeway, enters the County via the Berkshire Downs in the north-east and follows the chalk escarpment as far as the West Kennet Long Barrow. There are many other ancient hill top paths as well as the usual assortment of field paths, boundary paths, cart tracks, green lanes, old coach roads and quiet country lanes which offer the rambler almost unlimited opportunities for exploration and recreation.

To choose a dozen walks of around five miles from the wealth available presents a difficult task. However, I hope that the walks described in this book provide a representative slice of this beautiful county. All the routes use rights of way which I have checked with Wiltshire County Highways Department. The sketch maps together with the detailed descriptions should be sufficient to guide the walker on all these rambles, though the relevant Ordnance Survey 1:50,000 series maps will always prove informative and useful companions. Those sheets which include Wiltshire within their scope are as follows:

Sheet 173 Swindon and Devizes
Sheet 174 Newbury and Wantage
Sheet 183 Yeovil and Frome
Sheet 184 Salisbury and the Plain

No special equipment is needed to enjoy the countryside on foot but do remember that a muddy patch is likely to be encountered even on a sunny day. During a wet spell you are advised to wear shoes which are waterproof, if not wellington boots.

Good luck, and I hope you enjoy these walks as much as I did in preparing them for this book.

Roger Jones
January 1983

"Always get over a stile", is the one rule that should ever be borne in mind by those who wish to see the land as it really is — that is to say, never omit to explore a footpath, for never was there a footpath yet which did not pass something of interest.'
Richard Jefferies

KEY TO SKETCH MAPS:

Route along lane, road

Route along track

Route along footpath

River or stream
(arrows show direction of flow)

 Woods

+ + + + Railway

 Canal

 Water

Buildings

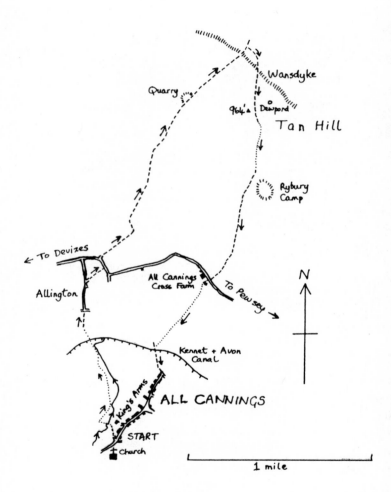

Wansdyke

Quarry

96l/2's   Dewpond

Tan Hill

Rybury
Camp

← To Devizes

All Cannings
Cross Farm

To Pewsey

Allington

N

Kennet + Avon
Canal

King's Arms

ALL CANNINGS

START

Church

1 mile

All Cannings
via Allington, Tan Hill, Wansdyke and Rybury Camp

Distance: 5 miles   **Time:** 2½ hours

The walk is based on the ancient and attractive village of All Cannings some four miles east of Devizes. The route follows field paths to cross the Kennet and Avon Canal and reach the hamlet of Allington, thence by a metalled track to ascend Tan Hill as far as the Wansdyke. The ascent of Tan Hill grows gradually steeper before levelling out as the summit is approached: the track takes you from around 400 feet to around 960 feet. You are then at the highest point in Wiltshire and there are spectacular views. From Tan Hill you descend steadily by field path and track past the Iron Age site of Rybury Camp and on to All Cannings Cross Farm on the main road, thence by field path to recross the canal and return to All Cannings. There is a good pub — The Kings Arms — in the village.

All Cannings is mainly arranged along a single street running parallel to the lane which branches off south from the main road between Devizes and Pewsey. The church of All Saints is situated towards the southern end of the village and set back a little from the road. There is a village green and playground here and room to park your car.

With your back to the church, bear right and take the first minor track on the left. This leads past the entrance drives of a number of houses to a small grassy area beyond the village pub. Continue in the same direction towards a footbridge over a stream. Cross the stile beyond into a field and head towards another stile in the fence opposite and slightly to the left. Now turn right and follow the field boundary and fence on the right for almost half a mile, until you are within 25 yards or so of the far corner of this large field. On your way through this field you can see the White Horse above Alton Barnes a couple of miles to the east. Look out for a gap in the hedge on the right: follow the path through the hedgebank and climb up onto the towpath of the Kennet and Avon Canal. Cross the wooden bridge and continue in the same direction by a path between fences.

You soon reach the lane beside the entrance to Allington House. Carry on by the lane, past the brick built Baptist Chapel, dated 1829, and branch off to the right along a grassy track beside ranch type fencing. This path leads to a lane where you turn left, past Allington Cottage, as far as a point where the road bears left. Here you turn right along a track signposted 'Bridleway Only'. Now you follow this track for almost 1½ miles as far as the Wansdyke. The ascent is at first gradual but later increasingly steep. The view east and south begins to open out: the chalk escarpment is here well marked and the hills seem to be rolling into the vale below or, alternatively, the corn fields in the vale appear to be lapping against the green slopes of the hills, like a gentle sea. You pass a small quarry in the hill side on the left which provides a good exposure of Upper Chalk, from which no doubt some fossil specimens could be extracted. As you crest the hill the wide view to the west and north presents itself.

Now you begin to descend slightly towards the Wansdyke: you reach a gate at the point where the track crosses the dyke. From here you can see the line of the Wansdyke heading away to the west, across the A361 and over Morgan's Hill. Go through the gate and turn right, up a stony track. Look out for an opening on the right by which you recross the Wansdyke to reach a gate on the far side. (If you reach a gate along the track signposted 'Private' you will have gone too far, so turn back and look for a way to recross the dyke).

The right of way now follows a fence on the right hand side as you head due south towards the summit of Tan Hill. You will see the Ordnance Survey triangulation marker in the field on the right: this marks the 964 feet summit — the path itself reaches 961 feet. This is, perhaps, the best point to take in the view. Tan Hill is at once the highest and most central point in the County and from it you can see more of Wiltshire than from anywhere else. I have been told that it is possible to see, on a suitably clear day, right across Pewsey Vale and Salisbury Plain to the spire of Salisbury Cathedral, near the southern boundary of the County. Closer at hand is Roundway Hill above Devizes, the Landsdown Monument to the north-west, Windmill and Silbury Hills to the north and the Marlborough Downs to the north-east. To the east you look down the wide and fertile Pewsey Vale.

Directly on your left is a regular circular depression — this is the remains of a dew pond, which were once a vital source of moisture on these otherwise waterless chalk downs. Go through the gate on the edge of the escarpment ahead. You now no longer follow the fence on the right hand side but head downhill by the footpath slightly to the left. Rybury Camp, with its encircling ramparts, is clearly visible on the hill below. Continue by the path towards a gate below the flank of Rybury Camp, then through a further gate to enter a field — here you follow the field boundary and the fence on the right hand side. You leave the field and continue in the same direction by a track between thorn trees towards All Cannings Cross Farm.

Cross the main road and head through the farmyard towards a gate to the right of a couple of houses. From here bear slightly to the left towards a second gate. Now follow the line of telegraph poles towards a gate in the far corner to enter another field. Head straight across this field towards the diamond shaped G.W.R. signpost giving weight restrictions of vehicles allowed to cross the bridge over the canal at this point. Once across the bridge continue by the track towards the village main street and the start of the walk.

All Cannings is as typically Wiltshire as you can get: a village neither small nor large though still very much a living village complete with three working farms, a church, school, post office/ shop and pub, set in rich agricultural country at the foot of lofty chalk hills only a few miles from Devizes, that most typically Wiltshire town. All Cannings is not outstandingly beautiful or charming but it is, nevertheless, most attractive in its setting and in the diversity of the buildings to be seen in a perambulation of the long village main street. There are many half timbered cottages, usually with thatched roofs and brick infilling which is painted some light shade to contrast with the black timbers. More recent houses are generally red brick with red tile roofs, and sometimes have tile hung first floors.

11

All Cannings was, at the time of the Domesday Book, the most important place in this part of Wiltshire. Indeed, St James' Church in Devizes was a chapel of ease to All Saints in All Cannings. All Saints is a large church dominated by its central, Perpendicular, tower. Only fragments of the original Norman work remain and the rest of the fabric is a mixture of styles and ages. The chancel was rebuilt in 1867 by the rector, the Rev J.A. Methuen, as a memorial to his friend the poet Coleridge, who visited him here fifty years previously in 1817.

Tan Hill is, according to John Aubrey's account, a corruption of St Anne's Hill, and was the site of an annual fair held on St Anne's Day, 26th July (although later accounts have it that the fair was held on 6th August), when the chief commodities were sheep, oxen and fineries. Tan Hill Fair seems to have died out around the turn of the last century but what a splendid site this must have been for such an event: a spectacular meeting place for traders and revellers from all over the County.

The dew pond seen near the hill's summit is an example of a traditional method of gathering water on the dry, porous, chalk hills. A shallow pit was dug and lined with clay so that rainwater (rather than dew) would collect and not drain away, though much must have been lost through evaporation.

The White Horse cut into the chalk escarpment above Alton Barnes is the biggest of the Wiltshire White Horses and was cut in 1812.

Rybury Camp is a pre-Roman fortification on a southerly spur of Tan Hill. It was long thought to be an Iron Age hill fort with bivallate defences, though lately it has been suggested that the Iron Age constructions overlie an earlier camp of the Neolithic period. Beside the footpath less than half a mile south-east of Rybury Camp is the site of an Iron Age settlement which was excavated in 1920 and yielded evidence of dwellings and storage pits as well as much pottery and brooches which were dated to around 600 B.C.

Barbury Castle
via Ridgeway, Broad Hinton and Uffcott

Distance: 7¾ miles   **Time:** 3 hours

The walk, although longer than the others in this book, is neither tedious nor exhausting, but is an exhilarating one which describes the four sides of a square. The starting point is Barbury Castle Country Park where Wiltshire County Council has designated a triangle of downland for recreational use. This includes the well preserved Iron Age fort of Barbury Castle itself with its wide views over Swindon and the Vale of North Wiltshire. From here the route joins the Ridgeway Long Distance Path as it heads south westwards along the high ridge of Hackpen Hill. A short distance before reaching a white horse cut into the face of the escarpment, the route changes direction to descend the scarp face and reach the village of Broad Hinton. From here you follow a lane to the hamlet of Uffcott, then complete the fourth side to return to Barbury Castle.

There are two pubs at Broad Hinton: the Bell Inn is on the main road before you enter the village. This hostelry surely deserves an entry in the Guinness Book of Records for serving the most enormous Ploughman's Lunches — certainly I have never encountered such a gargantuan plateful! The Crown is in the village itself.

Barbury Castle Country Park can only be approached by a lane which heads south from the B4005 which connects Wroughton and Chiseldon, two villages south of Swindon. This lane is well signposted; it passes the RAF Hospital and crosses the Ridgeway path before ascending the chalk escarpment to reach the Country Park, where there is a very large car park. Leave your car and head for the small buildings at the western end. Here the County Council have erected a very useful photographic display on

13

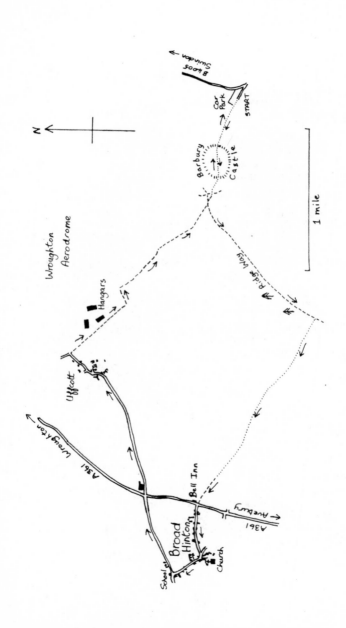

important features of the Marlborough Downs under the headings 'Geology, Landscape and Soils', 'Nature Conservation', 'Development of Agriculture', 'Prehistoric Life on the Downs', 'Hill Forts and their Conservation', 'Barbury Castle Country Park', 'Nearby Monuments' and 'Alfred Williams and Richard Jefferies'.

From here you go through the gate and follow the path through the field across the top of Barbury Hill, keeping the field boundary on your left. This ridge top path provides a magnificent view in all directions: ahead towards Barbury Castle, north over Swindon and south to the hinterland of the Marlborough Downs, with its large fields and smaller areas of grazing for sheep. Trees are planted in lines to act as windbreaks on these exposed uplands.

At the end of this field go through another gate to cross the impressively proportioned double ramparts of Barbury Castle. You leave the castle on the opposite side and begin to descend: from here you can see Broad Hinton to the west and the Hinton Plain spread out before you. The escarpment here only cuts through the Middle and Upper Chalk; the Lower Chalk and Upper Greensand form a second escarpment some two or three miles to the north west. Between these escarpments the Lower Chalk forms a kind of terrace, known as Hinton Plain. Wroughton Aerodrome is situated on this plain just to the north.

Below Barbury Castle the path reaches a gate — go through here and continue in the same direction. Ignore the signpost on the right indicating a public footpath to Uffcott and Broad Hinton but continue to follow the Ridgeway in its gentle ascent of Hackpen Hill. The Ridgeway here forms a boundary between parishes and this is marked by the sarsen stones acting as boundary markers beside the track.

Follow the Ridgeway past a clump of trees on your right to reach a high point of 883 feet. From here you have long views south across the Kennet Valley to the hills north of Pewsey Vale and south-westwards to Beacon Hill north of Devizes. After passing a second clump of trees you descend to reach a gap in the fence on your right. Enter the field here and descend the scarp face, keeping the field boundary on your right. You reach a gate and stile below — cross the stile and continue downhill in the same direction.

Follow a sunken path through the next field to reach a wide, grassy track between fields, heading in the same north-westerly direction. You pass some buildings to the left and the track turns to reach them: here you bear right and left to follow the hedgebank on your left. Carry straight on to reach the Bell Inn and the main road.

From the Bell Inn head towards Broad Hinton by the lane opposite the pub. When the lane reaches a thatched cottage bear left to reach the lych-gate which leads to the village church. On leaving the church bear left past The Crown pub, the shop and post office, towards the village school, then right back to the main road.

Cross over the main road and continue by following the lane opposite to Uffcott. Notice a fine curving thatched wall opposite the telephone kiosk. As you leave Uffcott the lane bears left to reach the main road once more; here you bear right along an unmade track beside three hangars belonging to Wroughton Aerodrome (how much less of an eyesore these hangars would be if their roofs were green instead of their present pale grey colour).

Once past the hangars, the right of way cuts straight across the field but respect for growing crops would suggest deviating from the right of way by following the clearly defined track to the left. When you reach a T-junction of tracks, turn right and head between fields and up the escarpment until you rejoin the Ridgeway. You now retrace your steps by bearing left and taking the right fork to the gate, then following the path up to Barbury Castle to return to the car park.

Barbury Castle is an Iron Age hill fort with fine double ramparts defending a hill top position at a point where the Marlborough Downs start to bend to the south. It encloses about 12 acres and there are traces of pits and hut circles. Any force advancing from the Thames could not have avoided Barbury Castle. The battle of Beranburh was an example of such a clash and took place in 556 in the plain just north of the Castle. Here the British attempted to repel the Saxons coming from the north. 'Beranburh' means Bera's Hill, and it is from this that the name Barbury Castle is derived.

The Ridgeway is a prehistoric road, now designated a long distance path which runs from Overton Hill south east of Avebury to follow the chalk ridge of the Marlborough Downs and the Berkshire Downs to the Thames at Streatley. From the opposite bank at Goring, the Icknield Way continues across the Chiltern Hills to Ivinghoe Beacon in Hertfordshire. At Barbury, the official Ridgeway cuts through the Castle and heads south-eastwards along Smeathe's Ridge to reach Liddington Castle via Ogbourne St George. The ancient road actually bypasses Barbury Castle to the north and takes a more direct line to Liddington via Chiseldon, though parts of this old route are now metalled road.

Broad Hinton church is dedicated to St Peter Ad Vincula and is Early English with a Perpendicular tower and all much restored a century ago. The church contains many monuments: just inside the door is a large and impressive one to Sir Thomas Wroughton who died in 1597 and his wife. Both figures are kneeling in prayer and below them are representations of their four sons and four daughters. The oldest of St Peter's monuments is a thirteenth century coffin lid with carving. This is in the chancel just to the left of the altar. In the chancel too, set into the wall, is the standing figure of Francis Glanville, killed in battle at Bridgwater in 1645 fighting for the Royalist cause. His armour hangs above the monument.

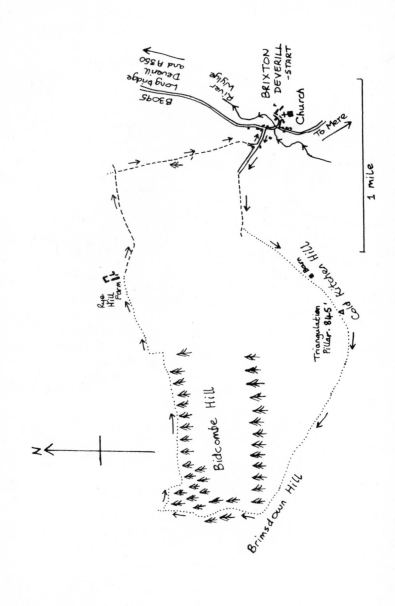

Brixton Deverill
via Cold Kitchen Hill and Bidcombe Hill

Distance: 6 miles   **Time:** 2½-3 hours

The walk starts in the delectable valley of the Deverills. The Deverills are five villages strung out over about three miles along a wide vale between chalk hills. They are, from north to south: Longbridge Deverill, Hill Deverill, Brixton Deverill, Monkton Deverill and Kingston Deverill. The combined population is not very great — less than 1,000. This route takes Brixton Deverill as its starting point and there are good views down to Kingston Deverill from Cold Kitchen Hill. None of the slopes are steep and the hill walking is most exhilarating, with wide views in every direction. Following the descent from Bidcombe Hill, there are several fields to traverse before reaching a green track which heads back to Brixton Deverill.

The only pub in the Deverill valley is 'The George' at Longbridge Deverill, where the minor road from Maiden Bradley meets the A350.

To begin the walk: With your back to the church at Brixton Deverill, walk to the main road and bear right, then take the first turning on the left. Once past Cliff House and some farm buildings on your right you go straight on and begin to climb by a chalky track. After about half a mile, as you lose sight of the village, the track levels out and begins to descend. Here you must change direction by bearing left. Pass the steel trough on your right and follow a barbed wire fence on your left to pass through a pair of steel gates to enter a field. Now simply continue in the same direction, gradually ascending all the time and with a fence a little way to your left. When a barn comes into sight, head towards it and there you will find a stile in the far left corner.

You are now on the last leg of the ascent of Cold Kitchen Hill. From the barn the right of way enters the field to the right, and heads diagonally across the field following a line of tractor tracks. As you progress further uphill, you will notice an area of uncultivated ground on your right — this marks the remains of a Long Barrow. Pretty soon you reach a triangulation pillar marking the 845 feet summit; this is a good position from which to take in the view. The woods of Longleat are prominent to the north, Arn Hill above Warminster marks the edge of Salisbury Plain, and due west is the isolated chalk hill of Little Knoll, followed by the extended ridge of Long Knoll.

The River Deverill rises below Little Knoll to become the River Wylye further downstream. This range of chalk hills to the north-west of the Deverill valley is, unlike much of Salisbury Plain which is occupied by the military, accessible to walkers and is typical of the county that so inspired Richard Jefferies and W.H. Hudson. Indeed it is a beautiful country, characterised by wide views, fields of waving corn, sheep in fields of closely bitten turf, huge skies and cloud shadows racing across the smooth, curving hills.

From the triangulation marker continue to follow the tractor tracks until you reach a fence on the left. Now follow the right of way with the fence on your left, below which you can see the church and houses of Kingston Deverill. You cross two stiles into successive fields and eventually reach a point close to the woods which grow on the slopes of Brimsdown and Bidcombe Hills where the fence and right of way take a turn to the right.

The right of way actually crosses the field on your right but in summer this field is usually waist high in corn. To avoid ploughing through these crops it is advisable to continue to follow the fence on the left towards the stile ahead. Do not cross this stile but bear right to follow the fence and woods on your left. You reach an iron gate by which you enter a wood. The footpath soon reaches a height of 918 feet which is only a few feet below the summit of Brimsdown.

You now start heading gently downhill. Continue to descend until you reach a gate at the edge of the wood. Go through the gate and bear sharp right to follow the edge of the wood on the right hand side. Pass through a gate, then a second gate and carry on until you reach the edge of the wood where you should head right towards a steel gate, beside which is a stile and a sign indicating Right of Way in either direction. Cross the stile and follow the fence on your left a short distance to reach the corner of the field to the left; bear left and follow the fence once more on your left until you reach a wide track between hedge-banks.

You approach Rye Hill Farm; this is the first habitation to be encountered since leaving Brixton Deverill. Continue ahead by the indicated right of way along the track to the right of the farm. When you reach a crosstrack marked by a bungalow away to the left, you bear right along what appears to be the broadest and most used track and ascend slightly towards woods. The footpath through the woods eventually reaches a crosstrack where you bear left towards Brixton Deverill, which soon comes into view. You join the track by which you began the walk just behind Cliff House. Here you bear left to reach the main road and the church again.

Brixton Deverill is really little more than a hamlet, but an attractive one. The church of St Michael is rather odd looking with a tower short and squat in relation to the pitched roof of the nave. The list of rectors dates from 1361 and the triple shafts of the chancel arch, as well as the lower portion of the tower, bear witness to the thirteenth century origins of this church. You enter by a door under the tower and the first object you encounter is the large Norman font decorated with a band of arrowheads below the rim. This font has been removed here from the church at Imber, the lost village of Salisbury Plain, used since the last war by the Army for shelling practice. Many of the houses in the Deverills are roofed with thatch and built of greenstone, the local building stone, the walls often being reinforced with brick courses.

According to the Oxford Dictionary of English Place Names, the word 'Deverill' has, unusually for this part of England, a Welsh or British derivation, and means 'the river of the fertile upland region'. John Aubrey, writing in the seventeenth century in his 'Natural History of Wiltshire', says that 'Deverill hath its denomination from the diving of the rill, and its rising again. In this shire is a small rill called Deverill, which runneth a mile under ground'. Whichever is correct, I think Aubrey's the more picturesque version.

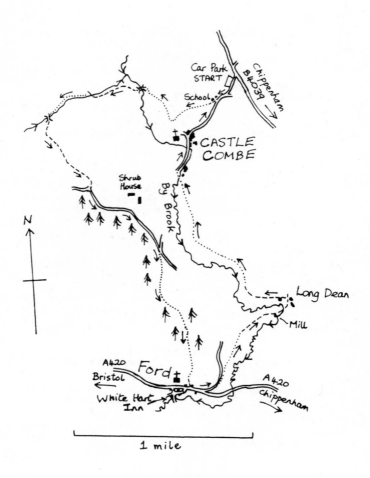

Car Park
START

Chippenham B4039

School

CASTLE
COMBE

Shrub
House

By Brook

N

Long Dean

Mill

A420
Bristol

Ford

A420
Chippenham

White Hart
Inn

1 mile

Castle Combe
via Castle Combe Park, Ford and Long Dean

Distance: 5 miles   **Time:** 2½-3 hours

The walk is an extremely pleasant one by well used and well signposted footpaths. From Castle Combe the route takes you through Castle Combe Park and along a charming tributary valley of the By Brook, then up a hill and along a ridge. It then descends to a second tributary which meets the By Brook at the hamlet of Ford on the Bristol-Chippenham road. You soon leave the main road by the lane to Castle Combe, then take field paths and an old track to the former mills and cottages at Long Dean, thence by a delightful hillside path the remaining mile to Castle Combe.

There is a fair amount of climbing on this walk but none of the slopes are steep and the hills, although their proportions give an impressive appearance, are never more than about 150 feet above the valleys. There is a pub and some good tea rooms in Castle Combe, and a useful pub at Ford, which is about halfway along the route.

As you approach Castle Combe by road, sign posts will direct you to the Free Car Park at the top of the village, or Upper Castle Combe. Leave the car park and begin to descend by the road to the old village. Look out for a minor track on the right which is signposted as a public footpath leading to Nettleton Shrub. You pass the school (a memorial stone indicates 'National School 1826') — still in use as such, and head for a pair of gate posts. Now cross the wooden stile ahead, not the tarmac path to the right.

You now enter the grounds of Castle Combe Park where the

23

right of way follows the fence on the left. After a short distance, the footpath leaves the fence and bears slightly to the right until it follows a course beside the stone wall on the left. Ignore a stile leading down to the left but continue to follow the stone wall until you reach its extremity: now you follow a fence down towards a stone bridge across a brook. Continue by the footpath as it swings to the right — there is a view down the valley here to the gables of Castle Combe Manor.

Follow the path towards the buildings ahead and cross the bridge over the brook. Pass through a huge old iron kissing gate, then left after the first building ahead, below a tall brick chimney. Now follow the footpath until you reach a low stone bridge across the brook. This bridge is built of massive stone slabs resting on stone piers and, as such, is reminiscent of the ancient clapper bridges of Dartmoor.

From this bridge you leave the valley and begin to ascend by a sunken track which opens out to a level path on the hill top. Continue by this wide path to the lane and bear left, past the entrance to Shrub House and on to a junction. The lane you have been following continues its way to Ford whilst the lane sharp left leads back to Castle Combe. Our route, however, is by footpath from here to Ford. The footpath is reached through a gate on the right a few yards beyond this minor junction. Once through the gate you bear sharp left along a signposted public footpath indicating Ford: 1 mile.

Follow the footpath initially through woods, then above the valley, keeping to the left hand side all the way. You soon reach a gate with a stile beside it — climb this and continue in the same direction. Look out for a notice near a large ash tree saying 'Please Keep to Footpath' with an arrow pointing ahead and downwards. At this point you begin to descend the hillside, not precipitately but gradually, towards a gap in the trees below. Once through the trees you reach a massive stone stile and footbridge over a minor stream.

The footpath leaves the bridge and climbs slightly to meet another footpath coming from the right and then bears left to head downstream. Follow the path as it leaves the field and enters some trees — you reach a fence on the left. As you approach the first houses of Ford, climb up the bank on the right and keep the fence on your left until you reach a wooden stile which drops you into a lane leading down to the main road. The little church built in 1897 is along the road on the right and the White Hart pub is on the far side and a little below the main road.

From the lane turn left and then first left by the lane to Castle Combe. After ascending somewhat, look out for a stile on the right with a public footpath sign indicating Long Dean. From the stile you head diagonally across the field until you meet a track on the far side. Now follow the track in the same general direction. The field narrows as you enter some trees. Pass a ruined barn on the left, go through a gate and begin to descend by a sunken track towards Long Dean.

You come first to a former mill on the right, below which is a mill stream and sluice gate. Follow the track across the bridge over the By Brook. Ahead is another former mill and you can make out the course of a mill stream as it crosses the track from right to left. Bear left, past Rose Cottage and follow the track which rises gently. The track soon bears left but you follow the public footpath to the right. As the path levels out you reach a gate and stone stile; climb the stile and carry on.

This footpath is attractively positioned half-way up the hillside overlooking the By Brook valley. Once past the former mill in the valley below, you will see the spire of Castle Combe church upstream. The path eventually descends to the level of the stream; you climb a stile and carry on to another gate and a footbridge over the By Brook to reach the road. Here turn right for the remaining short distance beside the By Brook back to Castle Combe.

Castle Combe lies among hills of Bath Stone topped with Forest Marble so that, geologically speaking, as well as in appearance, this village belongs very much to the Cotswolds. Castle Combe has stone cottages and gabled houses, a market cross and medieval packhorse bridge, a handsome manor house and, watching over all, a proud church tower. The village nestles beneath well wooded hillsides only a mile south of the M4 but a world away from the motorway age.

You may, like me, experience a feeling of *déjà vu* at the first sight of this village. Such a feeling may not be entirely unfounded because Castle Combe, the ideal English village, has featured on countless calendars and chocolate boxes, as well as providing a set for the filming of 'Doctor Dolittle', when it represented 'Puddleby-on-the-Marsh'. The inevitable popularity of Castle

Combe and the measure of commercialism which goes with it does not add charm to what is, after all, an ancient village in a splendid setting.

In the twelfth century, the Manor of Castle Combe passed to a Norman family, the de Dunstanvilles, who built a castle on a spur of land above the present manor house. The village church contains a monument displaying a crosslegged knight dressed in thirteenth century armour who is believed to be one of the de Dunstanvilles. By the following century, the village and the surrounding countryside was enjoying a booming wool and cloth trade and Sir John Fastolf, then lord of the manor, was responsible for the erection of new mills and cottages for his workpeople.

Castle Combe was, at that time, more of a town than a village, bigger even than Chippenham, with a weekly market and an annual fair. However, the diminutive By Brook could not supply the power required by larger machinery and by the seventeenth century John Aubrey noted, in his 'Natural History of Wiltshire': 'The most celebrated faire in North Wiltshire for sheep is at Castle Combe, on St George's Day, whither sheep-masters doe come as far as from Northamptonshire. Here is a good crosse and market-house; and heretofore was a staple of wooll. The market here now is very inconsiderable .... I have heard old men say long since that the market at Castle Combe was considerable in the time of the staple: the market day is Munday. Now only some eggs and butter, etc.' All wool and cloth manufacture had ceased by the 1820s and Castle Combe became depopulated.

Time should be taken to make a tour of Castle Combe. There is not as much interest or diversity here as at Lacock, for example, but even more charm. The church of St Andrew is very striking: it has an impressive Perpendicular tower with fine stone vaulting inside. Much of the rest of the church was rebuilt by the Victorians but in the original style. One exceptional feature is the chancel arch which contains three statues on each side which lean upwards from the point at which the arch begins to curve inwards to its apex.

Available in the gift shop in Castle Combe is an inexpensive booklet called 'Discovering Castle Combe', by Liz Tresilian, which makes a useful guide to a tour of the village.

Devizes
via Kennet and Avon Canal, Roundway Hill and Oliver's Castle

Distance: 6 miles   **Time:** 3 hours

The walk is a rewarding one which affords magnificent views over Wiltshire in all directions. The walk leaves the historic town of Devizes by a bridge over a restored section of the Kennet and Avon Canal to follow a long, straight track between fields known as Quakers' Walk. On reaching the hamlet of Roundway, the route follows field paths to ascend the south facing scarp of Roundway Hill, which is not too steep a slope. Roundway Hill is the site of a famous battle of the English Civil War. On reaching a track, the way levels out and the view east and north presents itself. Further on you reach the entrance to Roundway Hill Covert, a section of woodland which clings to the steep, west facing scarp and which is managed by the Forestry Commission. There is a nature trail and a picnic area open to the public.

Beyond the entrance to the woods is the projecting spur on which the ancient fortification of Oliver's Castle is sited. It is well worth making a detour to circumnavigate this windswept bastion, with its wide views west. Having done so, you descend by the cleft which distinguishes Oliver's Castle from Beacon Hill. At the bottom of the slope you turn south to follow the edge of a field lying below the chalk scarp, after which you follow a lane and fieldpaths to reach the Kennet and Avon Canal again.

To begin the walk, make for the large car park beside the Kennet and Avon Canal in Devizes. This can be reached by

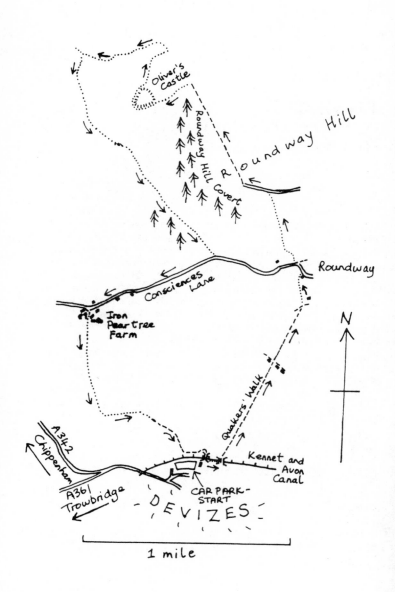

Oliver's Castle

Roundway Hill Covert

R o u n d w a y Hill

Roundway

Consciences Lane

Iron Pear tree Farm

Quakers' Walk

N

A342 Chippenham

A361 Trowbridge

Kennet and Avon Canal

CAR PARK START

D E V I Z E S

1 mile

Couch Lane from New Park Road, the road which bypasses the town centre and follows the medieval pattern of thoroughfares which form concentric circles, or semicircles, around the site of Devizes Castle. Facing the canal beside the Tourist Information Centre, bear right and follow the canal towpath under the first bridge and beyond until you reach a second bridge. At this point, climb up to the road and cross the bridge.

Once across the bridge you are faced with an impressive looking gateway: there are iron gates set between tall stone gateposts with a gatehouse on the far side. An opening on the right takes you to the driveway known as Quakers' Walk. You follow this straight track between hedgebanks and fields for about half a mile until you reach a lane flanked by modern bungalows. The lane leading away left is a private drive to Roundway House. Cross the lane and follow the unhedged track across fields on the far side. When you emerge at a lane below a house you bear left into a field opening and follow a fieldpath beside a row of telegraph poles. This takes you to a projecting hedgerow which you follow on your right. Once past the thatched cottage you reach a gap in the hedgerow through which you pass to reach the lane.

Now bear left and follow the lane as it swings sharply to the left below Roundway Hill. Just past the bend, look out for a wooden stile in the fence on your right. Cross the stile to enter a field, then head towards the far left corner where a second wooden stile drops you onto a field path across a wide open field on the slopes of Roundway Hill. You now begin to ascend by heading straight for the pylon ahead. Pass beside the pylon on the right and follow the fieldpath towards the hedgebank and fence directly ahead. Carry on in the same direction uphill until you reach a narrow metalled lane.

At this point you have almost reached the 700 feet contour and it is worth pausing to take in the view southwards before pressing on. The town of Devizes is clearly visible sited, as it is, on a plateau of Upper Greensand which includes the ridge of Caen Hill projecting westwards. Beyond Devizes and a little to the east is Echilhampton Hill and, beyond that, Salisbury Plain rises sharply from the Vale of Pewsey. Its western extremity is marked by the plume of smoke which rises from the cement works below the Westbury White Horse. On the north side of Pewsey Vale and in an easterly direction from this point are the Marlborough Downs and the peaks of Tan Hill and Milk Hill, both almost 1,000ft.

Continue the walk by following the lane as it rises a little further before levelling out on the summit of Roundway Hill. This straight track leads directly to Beacon Hill ahead. To its right is King's Play Hill, marked by a long barrow. Beyond King's Play Hill, to the north east, is Morgan's Hill with its copse of trees and twin masts below which can be seen the Wansdyke coursing across the summit. Roundway Hill forms the wide ridge running east-north-east. The lower land between these three hills was the site of an important battle in the Civil War.

Soon the metalled lane reverts to a dirt track. To the left, across the field, are the tree tops of Roundway Hill Covert, and soon you reach the entrance to the woods. Once past this point, the route bears left in order to take in the spur north of the woods. From here you follow the ramparts of the ancient camp known as Oliver's Castle. The hill falls away steeply on all sides but the east. From the westernmost tip of the ramparts you will surely stop to enjoy the prospect. In addition to many of the features already mentioned, there is a splendid view to the west and north-west. The low wooded hills to the north-west are comprised of Lower Greensand (here actually red rather than green) and, beyond them, Chippenham and the Vale of North Wiltshire. To the west, beyond the clay vale of West Wiltshire, rise the limestone hills of Cotswold.

The walk continues by following the high path beside the ramparts of Oliver's Castle and beyond until you reach an old iron gate. Pass through the gate and bear right to follow a fence on your right. At a second old iron gate bear left and descend by the footpath in the cleft below. Simply follow this wide track down beside the iron trough and across a sliver of arable land which intrudes into the chalk scarp to reach the far side and the continuation of the public footpath which follows the base of the scarp above a field. Look out for the boundary of the field on your left and, when you reach it, leave the footpath to enter the field. You now follow the right hand boundary of this field for over a mile in a south-easterly direction. You pass below the steep sided flank of Oliver's Castle and Roundway Hill Covert on your left. On your right are intermittent patches of woodland, the first of which conceals Mother Anthony's Well, a source of water which springs up at the base of the chalk hills.

On reaching the lane at an iron gate turn right until you reach

Iron Peartree and Rowde Field Farms. Between the farms on the left is a wide grassy area and a signpost indicating a public footpath to Devizes. Bear left and follow the way across the grass towards a point where the buildings converge. Soon you reach a stile; cross into the field and follow the hedgebank on the left. Cross a second stile and look out for a number of tree stumps carrying a wooden stile on the left. Cross here and head across the following field towards a point about 100 yards to the right of the house in the valley bottom. You will eventually spot a wooden stile in a slightly elevated position. Cross here to follow an overgrown track which soon reaches the drive to the house below. Continue the gentle ascent until you emerge from the drive to find a public footpath sign indicating that the way you have come leads to the curiously named Consciences Lane. Bear left at the cemetery and follow the Kennet and Avon the short distance to the bridge which leads directly to the Tourist Information Centre and car park from which you set out.

The Kennet and Avon Canal crosses the County from east to west and connects the Thames at Reading with the Bristol Avon at Bath. Construction began at Bradford on Avon and Newbury in 1794 and was not finished until 1810 with the completion of the Caen Hill flight of locks at Devizes. The canal enjoyed a period of reasonable prosperity until 1841, when the Great Western Railway line from London to Bristol was opened with its dramatic effect upon the fortunes of the Kennet and Avon and in 1852 the G.W.R. acquired the canal. Traffic dwindled to almost nothing by the 1920s. The future of the canal remained uncertain until the formation of the Kennet and Avon Canal Trust in the early 1960s. The Trust set out to restore the entire length of the canal. Much has been done, but much remains to be done, including the restoration of the formidable flight of locks which raises the canal up Caen Hill to reach the town of Devizes.

Roundway Hill was the site of a great battle in 1643 during the Civil War. The Royalist forces had suffered a defeat at Landsdowne near Bath and retreated eastwards, where they were pursued by Sir William Waller and his Parliamentary forces. When they reached Devizes, he laid siege to the town, but was repelled more than once when Lord Wilmot appeared with additional cavalry. Waller withdrew to Roundway Hill but soon descended and was attacked from both front and rear. He fled

31

while his forces surrendered. The hill was then named Runaway Hill by the Royalists, and this later became Roundway.

For those who wish to learn about the battle in more detail there is an excellent leaflet which can be bought from Devizes Museum in Long Street.

Oliver's Castle is a misnomer having its origin in the fact that it is near the site of the Civil War battle. It is in fact an Iron Age hill fort which was excavated in 1907 and yielded some fragments of pottery. The two small barrows to the south west of the perimeter date from the late Bronze Age (c. 1000 BC).

Holt
via Staverton, Whaddon, Broughton Gifford and Great Chalfield

Distance: 6 miles   **Time:** 2½-3 hours

The walk is an enjoyable and interesting one almost entirely by field and riverside paths through a pleasant countryside. This part of Wiltshire lies on the western edge of the clay vale, a landscape gently undulating rather than flat, lying between the chalk downs to the east and the foothills of the Cotswolds, 'the stone country', to the west.

Staverton marked an outpost of the once famous West of England wool and cloth industry and here a large water powered mill was built on the River Avon. At Whaddon we find a forgotten church set on a little promontory standing guard over a bend of the Avon. A little further north is an ancient pack-horse bridge, its sturdy stonework quite complete. The route touches Broughton Gifford at its southern extremity where the village church is situated. From there the route follows a bridlepath to Great Chalfield, a medieval manor which is one of the brightest architectural and historical gems of a county rich in such treasures.

There are shops and three pubs in the large village of Holt. There are no others directly on the route but short detours will take you to the Old Bear Inn at Staverton and the Bell Inn and Fox and Hounds at Broughton Gifford. There are some excellent spots for a picnic, for example near the packhorse bridge north of Whaddon.

The most attractive part of Holt is around the village green, or Ham Green, as it is known, at the south western end of the village. There is usually somewhere to park in the vicinity of Ham Green.

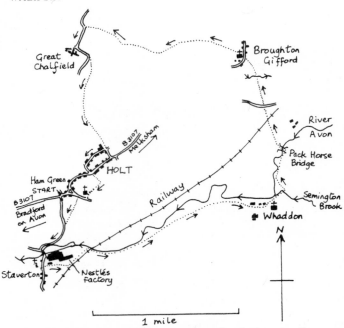

To begin the walk: leave Ham Green by the lane leading away from the main road towards the church of St Katherine. Directly opposite the gates to the vicarage you will see a public footpath sign by a kissing gate. Go through the gate to enter a field and head straight across the field towards the massive chimney of the Nestlés factory at Staverton. You cross an iron stile in the hedgerow ahead into a second field — from here you can see the weir above the mill stream just up river from the former mill. Carry on across the next field and bear a little to the right towards a gap in the hedgerow by which you reach the lane. Bear left, then left at the main road to cross the River Avon and walk past the factory on your left — notice the mill stream which still flows beneath the old factory building. Follow the pavement on the left up the rise to a point just beyond the ornate iron entrance gate to St Paul's Church opposite. This is an undistinguished building which came to this workaday community in 1826, two years after the Methodist Chapel. There is a pleasant view from the churchyard across the meadows beside the Avon towards Great Bradford Wood.

A few yards past a point opposite the entrance to St Paul's Church turn left along a track which leads past an attractive terrace of six factory cottages named 'Nasmilco'. Beyond the cottages the track reverts to a footpath between fences — the boundary fence of the factory on the left and, a little further on, the fence beneath the embankment of the railway line on the right. Follow the railway embankment until you reach the river, where you pass under the railway bridge to enter a field. Now leave the hum of the factory behind you and follow the right of way beside the river.

Cross one field boundary, then a second by a gate. In the third field the footpath follows a course which is elevated slightly above the immediate flood plain. The river bank is fringed by many crack willows and the flood plain provides an ideal habitat for moisture loving plants. Pass through another field boundary by a gate — now the river meanders some way to the left. Continue in the same general direction towards a gap in the hedge in the far boundary — you will see the bell turret of Whaddon Church beyond the farm buildings on the skyline ahead. Now plot a course through the middle of the next field towards a gate in the far boundary, then through a further gate. The footpath rises up the slope ahead towards Whaddon Farm — you should make for a point just to the right of the long, low sheds on the left. Leave the field by a gate on the left hand side, pass a pair of ruined cottages and head past a new bungalow towards the Church of St Mary, the key to which may be obtained at the bungalow.

To continue the walk: go to the north side of the church and follow the brick churchyard wall. There are trees and shrubs growing on the slope below — once past the trees head downhill by the grassy slope towards a rather elegant, arched, iron bridge over Semington Brook, a tributary which at this point joins the Avon. From here you bear slightly to the left towards a gate by the stone pier of the bridge which carried the former branch railway line to Devizes. Now head straight for the old stone pack-horse bridge.

Cross the bridge and bear half right to reach a stile in the fence above. You can see Monkton House to the right; this is a gabled stone house dating from the mid-seventeenth century. Continue in the same direction towards a stone stile set in a stone wall (the only one encountered on this walk). Cross here and head for the wooden stile beyond. This leads you across a single track railway to another stile opposite. Now make for a gate in the hedgebank ahead. Go through this gate, cross the road and climb a stile on the opposite side by which you enter a field. You can see Broughton Gifford Church directly ahead. Head across this field to a point just to the right of the clump of trees in the dip below. As you approach the field boundary you will see a wooden stile; this leads you across a footbridge over a brook to a second stile by which you enter one last field before reaching St Mary's Church. Follow the iron railings on the left towards a wooden stile on the lane beside the church.

Enter the churchyard by the gate and proceed beyond the tower to a stone stile, then go through an iron gate opposite to enter a field. Keep to the right hand side of the field, pass the buildings of Church Farm on the right to reach a gate in the far right corner. Head across the next field towards a gate in the hedgerow opposite. Go through this gate into a larger field and bear very slightly to the left towards a point just to the right of a clump of trees. Go through a gate into a further field and follow the hedgerow on the left towards a further gate and field and once again follow the hedgerow on the left. In the far left hand corner of this field you reach a wooden stile which takes you into a small narrow field. Walk through the middle of this field towards a stile in the far left hand corner. Cross here and follow the edge of the field beside a brook which runs below the hedgerow. You pass a pair of stiles and footbridge across the brook: this represents a short cut but the approach to Great Chalfield along the avenue from the north should not be missed. Carry on until you reach a gate on the left which leads to the avenue.

As you reach the Manor House turn left past the chapel beside the boundary wall and moat. The lane bears to the right at Mill Cottages; at this point enter the field ahead by a gate. Head across this field towards the corner before which you cross the brook by a wooden foot-bridge. Follow the field boundary beside the wood on the left, climb a stile and continue in the same direction towards another stile. Now follow the footpath through the field ahead and downhill towards the factory chimneys of Holt and, more immediately, towards a gate in the dip below. From here carry straight on through the narrow field ahead until you reach a stile and a track beside Sawtell's Bedding Factory. Now take the first on the right past the old brick and stone built factories. Keep your eyes peeled for an opening on the right where you will find a surprise: set in the factory wall is a pump between pilasters headed by an inscription commemorating the site of an old spa.

Carry on until the lane bears left at Beaven's Leather Works. At the main road cross over to continue by the footpath opposite. The Courts is the house behind the railings on the right and the gardens here belong to the National Trust and may be visited. At the end of this shady footpath pass through an iron squeezebelly stile to enter a field. Now bear right beside the boundary wall of 'The Courts' towards a kissing gate. Continue in the same direction where the path merges into a drive to a house until you reach St Katherine's Church. Bear right here along the lane which takes you back to Ham Green, where the walk began.

Holt has a complex of old industrial buildings which, together with some newer buildings, still house a significant industrial presence. The cloth factories have made way for the manufacture of bedding although the leather works, founded in the early 1700s, is still extant. The attraction of Holt as a spa was short lived though a pump remains as a reminder of more leisurely days. The church is a late Victorian rebuilding with the exception of the Perpendicular tower and porch. The house known as The Courts was so called because this was the place where weavers' disputes were settled.

Staverton is dominated by the Nestlés factory which has existed here since the turn of the century but which was formerly a cloth mill. There had been wool processing here from at least the sixteenth century but the present building, i.e. the two storey stone edifice below which the the mill stream runs, dates from 1824, the previous building having been destroyed by fire. Initially, the River Avon turned two water wheels but Staverton was to be the first mill in the area to install steam engines to drive the machines. Nestlés partly demolished the factory building in the 1930s by reducing the six storey mill to the present two. It was used as a milk condensary but now a whole range of processed foods are manufactured here. Nestlés was originally the National Anglo-Swiss Milk Co. and the terrace of workers' cottages seen on the walk are named 'Nasmilco' which is an acronym of that original title.

Whaddon The little church here is a surprise. It consists of nave, chancel, porch, chapel and bell turret. The chancel and bellcote are Victorian rebuildings. Medieval work remains in the nave, where there is a stairway in the wall beside the pulpit which once led to a rood loft, and in the carving to the doorway, also much restored. The Long Chapel contains two large marble monuments to members of the family as well as some lesser floor slabs. A flight of steps outside leads down to a tunnel-vaulted chamber dated 1778. The pack-horse bridge over the Avon to the north of the church is, I think, the finest of all the pack-horse bridges over the Rivers Avon and Frome in this area.

Broughton Gifford is a scattered community: the much restored church is at the southern tip of the village. The most memorable feature (not seen on this ramble) is the enormous, open common at the opposite end of the village. The houses surrounding the common are of all shapes, sizes and ages indicating the fact that this was a squatters' community where people came and exercised the right to settle. A Baptist Chapel was built here in 1806.

Great Chalfield This beautiful medieval manor belongs to the National Trust, has restricted opening hours but really must be visited. One of my favourite topographical writers, H.J. Massingham, saw Great Chalfield as the epitome of the country house of the resident native gentry, as opposed to the classically designed masterpieces of the absentee landlords which became the norm in a later era.

He writes* of such houses that, 'though a little withdrawn from (the countryside), they endow (the countryside) with an aristocratic quality without dominating it. Great Chalfield Manor, in north-west Wiltshire, built by Thomas Tropenell in 1490, with its grouping of farm, chapel, manor, mill, bartons and outbuildings, exquisitely shuffled together about a little flagged courtyard and surrounded by a little moat, with its tall square chimneys, wide gables, delicate oriels, crocketed belfry (to the chapel), great porches to the barns, carved finials at the ends of the broken facade, let Great Chalfield Manor in its radiant though reticent beauty stand as a concrete symbol of an ideal squirehood, so perfectly beautiful and moving it is embossed upon the fields and woods.'

*H.J. MASSINGHAM *The English Countryman* Batsford, 1942

Lacock
via Reybridge, Naish Hill and Bowden Park

Distance: 5 miles   **Time:** 2½ hours

The walk Lacock is probably the most beautiful and interesting of all Wiltshire villages. This route is a varied one using mainly field paths, but also including tracks and a short stretch of road. There are some splendid views from Naish Hill and Bowden Park. In addition, the route includes a section along the course of the long defunct Wilts and Berks Canal, and a stroll through the grounds of Bowden Park past the impressive house which looks westwards to the hills around Bath. There are several pubs and tea gardens in Lacock itself; 'The Bell' at Bewley Common beyond Lacock Bridge provides an alternative venue for a drink en route, particularly if Lacock is full of visitors. There is a pleasant garden, too, at this pub.

To begin the walk: take the lane leading north from the church and out of the village. You soon reach a footbridge and ford over the Bide Brook which flows just north of the village eastwards to join the River Avon. Lacock gets its name from this stream: 'Lacuc' is Old English for small stream. Once across the bridge you continue by the main path as it follows the brook to the right. You soon reach a house on the left where the track ends. Here you turn right and pass through a kissing gate to enter a field. Carry on by the metalled path across this field towards the houses below.

There is a wide view from this path, the most prominent feature being Naish Hill on the far side of the Avon. The lower slopes are

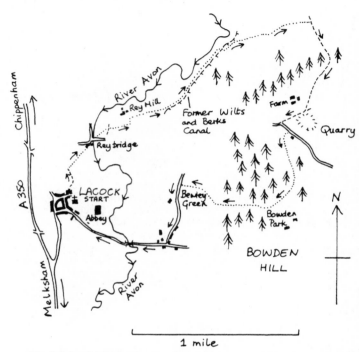

arable fields which rise to woods in the vicinity of Bowden Park
and Bewley Common.

You pass through a gate to reach the cottages and the road.
Bear right to cross Rey Bridge over the River Avon — note the
causeway, or flood walk, for pedestrians on the right. You climb a
stile immediately on the left to enter a field. Head diagonally
across this field to reach an iron squeezebelly stile about half-way
along the far boundary. Cross the drive here to the stile opposite;
the right of way now runs beside the fence on the left which is soon
joined by a fence on the right so that you are following a narrow
path between fences. You can see Rey Mill across the meadows to
the left.

You now cross a pair of squeezebelly stiles to enter a field. Head
diagonally to the left towards an opening by which you enter an

40

adjoining field on the left. Here you follow the fence and hedgebank on the right towards a ridge ahead. This represents the course of the towpath along the old Wilts and Berks Canal. The right of way follows the towpath on the left bank of the canal. After a few yards, the shallow basin, usually flooded, becomes clear. You soon reach a stile by which you enter a field. The bed of the canal is still visible, as is the towpath on the left.

You now reach a ruinous brick bridge over the course of the canal. Continue to the left of the bridge to reach a gate on the far side. Pass through this gate and cross the boggy canal bed towards another gate on the opposite bank. Bear left here and follow the overgrown canal on the left towards a gate into a further field. Continue in the same general direction across the field towards a fence in the far boundary; cross the fence and a short stretch of boggy ground to reach a fence into the next field. Ascend a little and, when the view becomes clear, head across the field just to the right of a large oak tree. Follow the hedge on the left beyond the oak tree towards a gate. Cross the next field and head towards a gate in the far boundary. Once through this gate follow a rough track beside a hedgebank on the left.

When you reach a metalled track running across your path, turn right and follow it to ascend the hill. You pass through some woods to emerge into some wide open fields where the track bears right; Ash Hill Farm is not far to the right. From Naish Hill there is a panoramic view northwards over the Vale of North Wiltshire — Chippenham is visible in the middle distance. To the west are the hills in the vicinity of Bath.

Follow the track as it takes another bend to the right; Naish Hill Quarry is on the left. This quarry is still worked for sand. The ground being excavated can be seen to yield boulders of ironstone as well as quantities of sand of a deep, rust-red colour. This ferruginous sand belongs to the somewhat misleadingly named Lower Greensand formation.

Turn sharp left at the lane ahead, past the entrance to Naish Hill Quarry and on towards the buildings ahead. Just before the first cottage cross the fence on the right to enter a field. Follow the hedge on the left to reach a stile. Cross into the next field. You must head diagonally up and across this field to reach a gate and stile in the top left hand corner. Now follow the fence on the left and shortly reach a gate by which you enter some woods. Follow the path through the woods and bear right at a crosstrack towards a gate and stile to enter a field. Follow the wood on the right until you reach the edge of the woods and a stile on the right. Cross the stile and begin to descend the field ahead.

There is once again a spectacular view to the north and west. The big house on the left is Bowden Park and, as you descend, its impressive features become more apparent. Continue downhill towards the trees on the right to the bottom right hand corner where you will find a gate and stile. Climb the stile and continue to descend through the next field towards a further stile. You can see Bewley Court straight ahead and, beyond that and slightly to the left, the chimneys and roofs of Lacock Abbey.

Continue in the same direction towards a further gate. From here you bear right to reach the bottom corner of the field. Cross the stile here and reach the next field: here you follow the hedgebank on the right to reach a stile. Once through the trees the path opens out onto a common and lane ahead. This is part of Bewley Common and belongs to the National Trust. Bear left to reach the lane and continue by this, past the ancient and attractive Bewley Court to reach the road. Bear right here ('The Bell' pub is to the left), cross Lacock Bridge over the Avon and the pedestrian causeway, pass Lacock Abbey across the meadows to the right and continue by the road until you reach the village again.

Lacock The National Trust owns Lacock Abbey, the Fox Talbot Museum of Photography and much of the village. A day could be fully employed in visiting the attractions of Lacock.

The village is described in the Domesday Book of 1086 but grew largely with the founding of the Abbey in the thirteenth century. In that century, too, a weekly market and an annual fair was established, and Lacock became an important centre, particularly in the trade and manufacture of wool and cloth. The nineteenth century witnessed a period of decline and the Victorian era of industrialisation bypassed Lacock with the happy result that the village's considerable stock of buildings from the thirteenth to the eighteenth centuries remained virtually intact: the village school of 1824 and after is one of the few nineteenth century buildings. Ownership by the National Trust has ensured that the many original and interesting buildings of this sizeable village are well conserved. Available in the National Trust shop is a booklet published by the Lacock Village Hall Management Committee entitled 'A Guide to Lacock'. This modestly priced publication makes an ideal companion to a perambulation of the village.

The Wilts and Berks Canal is described in Bradshaw's 'Canals and Navigable Rivers', published in 1904, as follows: 'Although the canal is officially closed, navigation throughout the whole of the system has practically ceased owing to the income being insufficient to meet the cost of maintenance'.

The Wilts and Berks was built under an Act of Parliament of 1795 from Semington on the Kennet and Avon Canal in Wiltshire to Abingdon on the River Thames in Berkshire, a length of 52 miles. In addition, there were several branches along its course. The canal was never a through waterway from Bristol to London, but rather an agricultural canal which served to carry coal from the Somerset Coalfield through Wiltshire to the Vale of the White Horse and agricultural produce from the country to the towns. The Wilts and Berks was expensive to build and only enjoyed a moderate prosperity before suffering the onslaught of the railways. Despite considerable reinvestment and successive attempts to revitalise the canal, it gradually faded into oblivion and was practically defunct by the turn of the century.

Bowden Park, completed in 1796, was designed by the architect James Wyatt (also responsible for William Beckford's Fonthill) for a rich Bristol merchant. From the footpath you can see the tall windows and stone walls of the north front and, as you descend, the elegant two storey bow of the west front, complete with four huge Ionic columns.

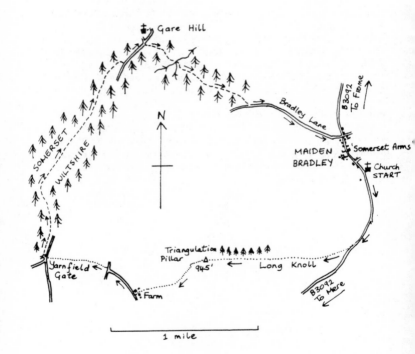

Gare Hill

SOMERSET
WILTSHIRE

N

Bradley Lane

B3092
To Frome

Somerset Arms

MAIDEN
BRADLEY

Church
START

Yarnfield
Gate

Triangulation
Pillar
△
945'

Long Knoll

Farm

B3092
To Mere

1 mile

Maiden Bradley
via Long Knoll and Selwood Forest

Distance: 6 miles **Time:** 2½-3 hours

The walk is mainly by field paths and forest tracks but includes a little road walking. There is much variety in the countryside traversed as well as some spectacular views. The route includes the ridge top path which courses along the top of Long Knoll and a forest track following the crest of the escarpment which forms a physical as well as administrative boundary between Wiltshire and Somerset.

The section of the walk through the forest from Yarnfield Gate to Gare Hill is actually in Somerset, although the track runs parallel to the county boundary which is only a few yards away. There is no village or roadside pub on the route of this walk: the hamlet of Gare Hill possesses only a redundant church and a few scattered cottages. There is a pub in Maiden Bradley, 'The Somerset Arms', which serves a good range of snacks and meals at lunch time. There are many excellent places for a picnic on this walk, in particular along the stretch through the woods beyond Yarnfield Gate.

To begin the walk: with your back to the church bear left, in a southerly direction, along the B3092 towards Stourhead and, more immediately, towards the twin hills of Little Knoll and Long Knoll. These isolated chalk ridges are aligned on an east-west axis and the road rises to a point between the two. As you approach the eastern tip of Long Knoll, bear right into a small wooded area where you will find a public footpath sign indicating the right of way to Kilmington via Long Knoll, and pointing into the trees.

The track through the woods soon reaches a wooden stile where you enter an open field and climb the steep slope to the ridge top path. Now follow the barbed wire fence on the right and continue to do so for almost a mile until making the descent of Long Knoll following the high point of 945 feet marked by a triangulation pillar. To reach this point you must cross a stile.

The view from the pillar is far and wide in every direction, as indeed it has been all the way along the ridge, except where obscured to the north by Long Knoll Wood. You can see woods to the west and north, Maiden Bradley to the north-east and Cold Kitchen Hill and Brimsdown to the east. To the south-west, embedded in a wooded hill, you can see Alfred's Tower, which has stood in that place since 1766.

From the triangulation pillar you descend the steep slope to the bottom corner of the field. The right of way crosses into the next field at this point, but two barbed wire fences and, in summer, a great mass of nettles, may deter you. A reconnaissance of the ground here suggests that ramblers have been crossing at a point about 20 yards to the left below an ash tree in the hedgerow. From here you make for a projecting corner of an adjacent field below and a little to the left. Now follow the hedgebank on the left towards the farm buildings. As you enter a further field by a stile, follow the line of isolated trees. Just before the buildings bear right then left through the farm buildings to reach the lane. Now bear right to reach a minor junction. Cross the road to reach the barbed wire fence opposite. From here the right of way is by a field path; cross the stile here to follow the hedgebank on the right. You cross a further two stiles before reaching the lane at Yarnfield Gate.

Cross the road and take the lane signposted to Witham Friary. Bear right at the cottage on the right and follow the signposted footpath to Gare Hill. Cross one gate and then follow a rough track through woods. Quite soon the track opens out where the forest has been cleared on the slope on the left and there is a long view west into the heart of Somerset. This impressive sloping of the ground away to the west marks the greensand escarpment, where the Cretaceous strata of Wiltshire give way to the more ancient rock formations of Somerset. The predominance of bracken, rhododendrons and pine forest indicates the presence of an acid, sandy soil.

The track now forks: Take the right fork flanked by

rhododendron bushes. You eventually meet a cross track which you cross to continue in the same north-easterly direction along a flint strewn track. You reach another fork: again bear right to reach a lane. At the lane bear left to reach Gare Hill. Just before the lane swings left below Gare Hill you will notice a pair of public footpath signs indicating footpaths to the right. You take the second one, signposted to Bradley Lane, but first you may like to carry on to Gare Hill and its redundant Victorian church, from whose churchyard you might enjoy one last, splendid view over Somerset.

Follow the footpath towards Bradley Lane. To do so you must first descend to a stream, where the running water has created a valley by eroding the greensand to reach impervious clay strata beneath. The boggy habitat here is marked in the summer months by a vigorous growth of horsetail and water dropwort. Ascend the track, taking the right fork, on the far side of the stream as far as Bradley Lane where you bear left and continue until you reach the main crossroads in Maiden Bradley.

Selwood Forest: The woods along the Wiltshire-Somerset border represent the vestiges of the once substantial area covered by Selwood Forest, which formed a great arc stretching from the southern fringes of Bath in a southerly direction along the Wiltshire-Somerset border and into Dorset. Selwood Forest was an important factor in the history of southern England, acting as a barrier against successive waves of invaders from the east. These included the Celts who reached as far as West Wiltshire before the Romans invaded, and the Saxons, whose advance westwards after their victory at the Battle of Dyrham in 577 was checked not only by King Arthur's campaigns, but also by the existence of this great forest. It was not until 658 at the Battle of Penselwood that the Saxons finally broke through into the heart of Somerset.

For many decades, therefore, the Forest of Selwood formed the boundary between the Saxon Kingdom of Wessex and the British tribes in the West. And even today, this Wiltshire-Somerset boundary seems to me to constitute the most convincing dividing line between the otherwise rather nebulous regions referred to as 'Wessex' and the 'West of England', the chalk uplands and wide clay vales on the one side, and the more broken, hilly country on the other.

47

Maiden Bradley is a pleasant village with most of its grey stone buildings clustered around the crossroads and triangle of green at its centre, although the village 'main road' stretches half a mile south to the church of All Saints. The church is of interest more for its historical associations than its architectural splendour. Most impressive is the large monument to Sir Edward Seymour, Speaker of the House of Commons, who died in 1707. The elegant figure of Sir Edward is carved in white marble and he is seen resting on one elbow.

Inside the church there is a plaque commemorating Sir Edmund Ludlow, perhaps Maiden Bradley's most famous son. Ludlow was born in 1617. He took Wardour Castle in the Civil War and rose high in the Parliamentary army. He was a committed republican and was a member of the court which tried the King and signed his death warrant. Ludlow was bitterly opposed to Cromwell's dissolution of the Long Parliament and was eventually exiled to Switzerland where he died and was buried. The most surprising object in the church is in the shape of a human skeleton, on full view, but I will leave that for you to discover yourself.

The place name 'Maiden Bradley' has an interesting derivation. 'Bradley' is a common English place name, meaning literally 'broad leigh', i.e. the broad clearing in the woods. 'Maiden' is most likely derived from one Maiden Bissett, who founded a hospital for leper maidens in the twelfth century. This became a priory, the scanty remains of which are now incorporated into the outbuildings of Priory Farm just to the north of the village.

Old Sarum
via Stratford sub Castle and River Avon

Distance: 3¼ miles   **Time:** 1½-2 hours

The walk is short, undemanding and packed with interest. The ancient hill top settlement of Old Sarum is the starting point for this walk which could well be coupled with a visit to the ancient monument. The route follows a number of green tracks and footpaths as well as a quiet stretch of lane. There are many interesting buildings in the village of Stratford sub Castle which is almost, but not quite, merged with the Salisbury suburbs.

There is a car park within the outer ramparts of Old Sarum which makes a convenient starting point for this walk. This is reached by a signposted track from the A345 Salisbury-Amesbury road, almost opposite the Old Castle pub. The outer ring and ground plan of the cathedral may be inspected from here and the remains of the castle in the inner ring may be seen on payment of a small entrance fee.

With your back to the entrance to Old Sarum bear left and follow the metalled track below the outer bank. As the track turns away to the right to reach the main road you bear left along the public footpath signposted to Durnford. Follow this green track with the outer bank of Old Sarum on your left and a wide view over fields towards the tree plantation on Little Durnford Hill a mile or so to the north-west. To the north-east the wide and shallow valley of the River Bourne gives way to the gentle chalk hills of Porton and Boscombe Downs. Looking ahead the land dips gradually to meet the Salisbury Avon.

Bear left at the lane below; when the lane swings to the right,

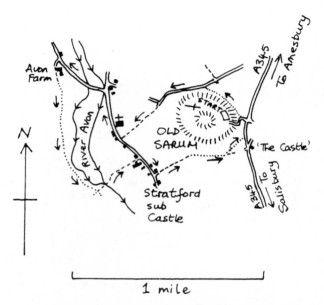

1 mile

continue in the same direction by a narrow, sunken and tree lined track which is signposted to exclude entry by motor vehicles except for access. Eventually the view opens out and you can see across a meadow on your left towards the spire of Salisbury Cathedral. On the right you will discover the stone and flint chequered walls of Stratford sub Castle church coming into view. The end of the footpath and the village high street are heralded by a pair of venetian windows under a gable. These belong to the eighteenth century Prebendal House. Bear right and walk past the twin projecting gables of an ashlar fronted house of an earlier century. This was once the vicarage and before that was the home of the Pitt family, the first William Pitt having been born here. This diminutive village was also the home of Lady Nelson.

Enter the churchyard of St Laurence by the iron gate beside the pavement. From the church continue along the lane in a northerly direction. At the junction you bear left by a bridge across the Avon. There are sluice-gates below the bridge to regulate the flow, much of which is diverted into a channel at the side. The river level downstream is considerably lower than upstream; the waters appear to be brimming to the edge of the flat and low lying meadows which form its flood plain. A short distance to the right may be seen the brick chimneys, stone gables and mullioned windows of Stratford sub Castle Manor House. Follow the lane as it crosses the channel diverted from the river to a point where it meets another channel. These numerous channels once fed the water meadows for which these valleys were ideally suited. You can see the remains of the former water meadows in the sculpting of the meadows all around here.

The farms hereabouts look particularly solid and prosperous, even in a county long renowned for its agricultural prowess. This Avon valley, like that of the Wylye, was beloved of Cobbett, who saw in it a fat and productive land employing all the latest techniques. As you approach Avon Farm Cottage you must change direction but first notice the variety of building materials of which this old cottage is composed. The walls are a mixture of greenstone, clunch, brick and flint, whilst the main roof is thatch and a side addition is tile. To add to the variety hereabouts you can count the stone and flint chequerwork walls and several examples of thatched wall, the thick cob walls protected by a generous and overhanging layer of thatch.

Turn sharp left up the track signposted to Avon Farm. The track skirts the farm buildings on the left and reaches a field by a gate. Enter the field and follow the hedgebank on the left. To your left, beyond the meadows, is the elegant tower of the Church of St Laurence and, behind it, the bosky slopes of Sarum Castle. You reach a stile in the far corner of the field; cross here and follow the path between fences. Cross a second stile and follow the footpath, slightly elevated above the meadows to your left and following the hedgebank on the right. Cross a third stile and follow the path until you reach a metalled cross path. To the right on the hill-top loom serried ranks of suburban semis. Straight ahead is the city of Salisbury with the spire of the cathedral dominating all, if such a pure and sublime edifice as Salisbury Cathedral's spire could ever be said to dominate its surroundings. The city seems very close although we are actually still in the country.

Turn left to cross the footbridge over the River Avon, the waters of which are wide, shallow, clear and swift flowing. Follow the footpath until you reach the village high street. There is a shop to the left beyond the cottage dated 1703. Turn right by the brick wall of Parsonage Farm. Beyond the farmyard is a plain, late Georgian farmhouse. Beyond that is a thatched wall, then a black and white half-timbered building standing opposite one built of flint with brick courses. Once past these you turn left by a bridleway signposted to Old Sarum. Follow the bridleway as it climbs gently towards the outer bank of Old Sarum — to the right are wide views over Salisbury. What a relief it is that the town planners have not allowed any high rise buildings to spoil that awe-inspiring vision of the cathedral!

Cross a stile to bear slightly to the right and follow the hedgebank on the left. Cross a second stile and head slightly to the left until you reach the main road where you follow the footpath directly back to the entrance to Old Sarum and its car park.

Church of St Laurence. Inside, the church is an unusual conglomeration of periods and styles. The font is Norman, the chancel early thirteenth century but containing much woodwork of Thomas Pitt's time; the nave is perpendicular and is surmounted by a wagon roof with bosses and supporting demi-angels; the pulpit is an impressive Jacobean example with sounding-board and hour-glass. On the wall beneath the gallery are three beautifully executed panels of illustration and script recounting the story of the church and explaining features of interest.

Stratford sub Castle's famous son, the first William Pitt, was the grandson of Thomas Pitt who made his fortune as an East India merchant. He bought the manor here in 1690 and became a considerable benefactor to Stratford's church: this fact is evidenced by the inscription in large letters on the church tower 'Tho. Pitt Esq. Benefactor'.

Old Sarum. Like Avebury and Stonehenge, it is difficult to do justice to Old Sarum in the space of a few lines. In contrast to those other two well known Wiltshire antiquities, Old Sarum does not represent a prehistoric site which fell into disuse with the arrival of the Romans. Rather it was used for a mixture of military, religious and settlement purposes by successive waves of new arrivals.

The hill top position was fortified during the Iron Age and later occupied by the Romans, if slightly, as a military station. It was named Sorbiodunum by the Romans. The Britons followed the Roman withdrawal, and they in turn gave way to the Saxons in 552; in 1060 Edgar held a council here. The Danes pillaged and burnt it in 1003 and Canute is said to have died here in 1035. An ecclesiastical settlement was started when a convent was founded in Edward the Confessor's time, and in 1072 the episcopal see was transferred here from Sherborne.

With the Normans, William the Conqueror granted Sarum to his kinsman Osmund. Osmund took holy orders, became bishop and finished building his cathedral here in 1092; it was extended and largely rebuilt by Bishop Roger following damage caused by a thunderstorm. At the same time however, the Normans were building their castle. Church and army did not mix and contemporary accounts tell of soldiers harassing the clergy until, in 1331, the cathedral at Old Sarum was forsaken and the materials transported to the site of New Sarum and the cathedral rebuilt there. When the cathedral moved so did the civilian population whose shops and houses had crowded together between the inner ring of the castle and the outer ring which still contains the ground plan of the cathedral.

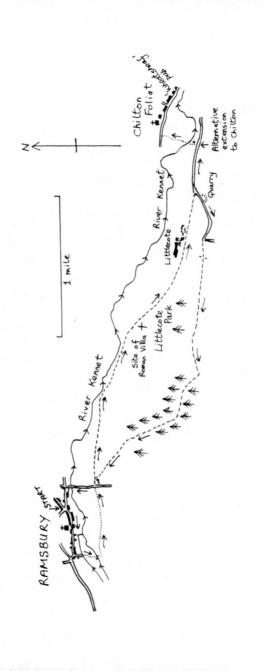

Ramsbury
via River Kennet and Littlecote House
(Optional extension to Chilton Foliat)

Distance: 6 miles or 8 miles   **Time:** 2-4 hours

The walk passes through quiet and unspoilt country, much of which is in the environs of the beautiful Elizabethan manor of Littlecote which lies low and secluded in the valley of the River Kennet. Littlecote House and its attractions including the Roman mosaic within its grounds are well worth a visit; details of opening times are in the notes at the end of the walk. Ramsbury itself is one of the most attractive large villages in the county.

The route follows a well made green track which is later metalled along the Kennet valley as far as the entrance gate to Littlecote. It then follows a lane to climb a gentle hill to return by the south side of the Kennet valley. This hill country is an attractive mixture of arable and woodland and no settlement is encountered until you emerge from the wood to meet the gorgeous prospect over the Kennet Vale to Ramsbury and the hills and patches of woodland beyond.

From the turning point at the gates to Littlecote it is possible to walk on for about a mile: in this case you cross the River Kennet by an attractive wooden bridge and head through a wood by a footpath to reach the village of Chilton Foliat. Here you are almost on the Berkshire boundary. Chilton is a quiet and pleasant village and the Wheatsheaf pub provides a good place of refreshment if you are one who requires a half way house. Alternatively, the crossing point of the River Kennet would provide a pleasant spot for a picnic.

The village of Ramsbury is situated just off the A419 road between Swindon and Hungerford. It is also easily accessible via a minor road from Marlborough. The best place to park and start the walk is in The Square; this is the natural focal point of the village. From here you head along the High Street in a westerly direction. You will soon pass the lych gate leading to the large church of the Holy Cross. Continue along the High Street: when you reach the end of the village you will observe a sign indicating 'To Footpath and Bridleway' and pointing to the left. Follow Mill Lane to reach a footbridge across the River Kennet. A few yards upriver from the bridge can be seen sluice-gates which controlled the flow of water to the mill. Half a mile to the west you can glimpse the impressive gates to Ramsbury Manor. Cross a second footbridge and continue by a footpath to pass between the cottages ahead. Immediately past the cottages on the left you take the footpath on the left which follows a straight course between the water meadows beyond the hedgerow on the left and the gentle grassy slope of Spring Hill on the right. Ramsbury can be seen on the far side of the valley, the grey church tower contrasting with the predominant red brick and tile of the vernacular buildings.

Cross the road ahead and follow the right of way on the far side, now a green track rather than a footpath. The bridleway signposted to the right and leading obliquely up the hill towards woods represents the last leg of this ramble. You approach a curious looking house and pass through a gate to follow a track in the same general direction by the River Kennet. The track now passes the site of a Roman villa which contains the famous Orphens mosaic rediscovered in 1977; see the notes at the end of the walk.

The major Elizabethan mansion of Littlecote can now be seen ahead, its red brick walls, gables and mullion windows lying intimately with the river, the meadows and the gentle wooded hills either side. You simply follow the track as it leads to the right of the house, past the great hall and the twin gables and porch of the south front, and on by the long avenue of lime trees to the entrance gate. If you have the time, a visit to Littlecote House itself is warmly recommended.

From the entrance gate you can bear sharp right to begin the return to Ramsbury or continue for a further mile to reach Chilton Foliat. If the latter is your intention, press on by the lane ahead until you reach a signpost indicating a public footpath to the left. Follow the path beside the boundary hedge of a house and its grounds on the right. You soon reach the River Kennet which is one of those wide and clear streams typical of the chalk country; here I saw swans and a Canada goose. On the opposite bank continue by the footpath through the wood until you reach the road where you bear right to reach the village. The church of St Mary is on the left, then an elegant Georgian house once the rectory.

Back at Littlecote Manor entrance gate press right on to follow the lane up the hill. Quite soon on your left is a rock face exposed in a small quarry working. This is a section through chalk strata showing bands of flint. The soil and subsoil appear to penetrate quite deeply into the bed rock. Further on the lane bears sharply to the left. At this point carry straight on through a gate signposted 'Littlecote Park'; now follow the metalled track through woods and past the jousting arena, and a felon hanging on a gibbet. Where this track swings to the right down towards the visitors car park continue straight ahead along the track indicated 'Private – No Through Road'. After reaching a crosstrack you descend slightly until you reach a double row of stately beeches which you pass on your right. At the end of this row of beeches the track forks – take the right fork and gradually ascend.

At a point where the metalled track swings sharply to the right you follow a footpath through the woods directly ahead. This track begins to descend until it emerges from the trees to present an inspiring view across the Kennet valley towards Ramsbury and the gentle hills beyond. Follow the track down until you reach the road and the bridge across the river and into the village. Bear left at 'The Knap' and follow the lane until you reach The Square again where the walk began.

Ramsbury is a large village in the valley of the River Kennet which bisects much of the Marlborough Downs from west to east. It is not strictly a linear village, though its streets and buildings are inevitably arranged about an axis which corresponds to the valley. Ramsbury's buildings are mainly of red brick but there are some older, half timbered and thatched cottages and there were a great many more before a series of fires took their toll.

The church is built of flint and its massively buttressed tower rises above the predominantly red brick village. The church of the

Holy Cross is a large and imposing structure, both inside and out. The present building dates from the thirteenth century; the aisles were added in the following century. The church was heavily restored in the 1890s when the aisles were rebuilt and enlarged. During the course of building operations many fragments of carved stone were unearthed and were recognised as belonging to the original Saxon building. These fragments are now on display in a corner of the church. Ramsbury constituted a bishopric in Saxon times. Between 909 and 1058 the Bishop of Wiltshire resided at Ramsbury; after 1058 he moved to Sherborne and in 1075 Old Sarum became the see city of the enlarged diocese, which included the counties of Wiltshire, Dorset and Berkshire. A board on the wall opposite the door lists the names of the old Bishops of Ramsbury. The bishopric was restored in 1975 with the appointment of a suffragen bishop intended to assist in the Wiltshire division of the large Salisbury Diocese.

Littlecote is a splendid brick built mansion dating back to the fifteenth century though essentially Elizabethan in appearance. The core of the building consists of an E-plan but the porch and twin gables are well spaced and do not project far.

Littlecote came into the possession of the Darrell family in 1415 and passed to Sir John Popham in 1589, and the manner in which it did so is curious. John Aubrey, writing in the seventeenth century, was the first of many to recount the sequence of events. He tells how Will Darrell had got his wife's maid pregnant and called for a midwife, one Mother Barnes, to attend her during childbirth. The midwife was brought blindfolded, delivered the baby, whereupon Will Darrell threw it on the fire to destroy it. He paid Mother Barnes and sent her away, again blindfolded. The good midwife's conscience troubled her and she went to the local magistrate and eventually Littlecote was discovered to be the scene of the crime and Will Darrell the perpetrator. Darrell was brought to trial before Judge Popham who, says Aubrey, acquired Littlecote as a bribe to save Darrell's life. Within a year Will Darrell was killed falling from his horse.

There are many inconsistencies between Aubrey's account and historical facts but the root of the story, that a newborn baby was murdered by Will Darrell at Littlecote, remains. There are, of course, many reports of ghosts of mother, baby and midwife being seen at Littlecote and of Darrell where he fell from his horse.

The house contains a wonderful collection of furniture and works of art. Of particular interest is the display of arms and armour from the Civil War period belonging to the house, and still displayed in its original setting within the Great Hall. Following the recent acquisition of Littlecote by Mr Peter de Savary many new attractions have been added for the visitors to enjoy. These include joustings, a 17th century village, falcanry and a riverside railway. Littlecote is open to the public daily from Easter to the end of October.

The Roman mosaic on the villa site adjoining Littlecote House was first discovered in 1725 but was reburied intact by the owner of the property to avoid publicity. It was rediscovered in 1977 and excavations over the whole villa area of some three acres have continued ever since. The mosaic has now been restored and relaid. It was probably constructed around 360 A.D. and its importance lies partly in its sheer size, partly in its religious associations through its central character of Orpheus, and partly in the building which originally housed it whose plan conforms more to a typical sixth century church of Byzantium than of Rome.

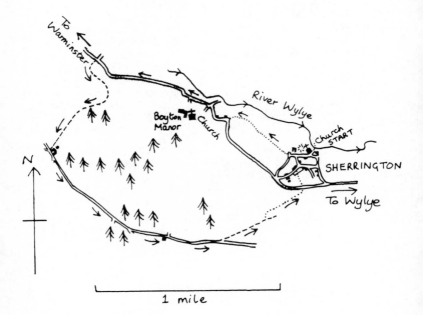

To Warminster

River Wylye

Boyton Manor

Church

Church START

SHERRINGTON

To Wylye

N

1 mile

Sherrington
via Wylye Valley, Boyton, Corton Hill and Boyton Down

Distance: 4 miles   **Time:** 2½ hours

The walk is based on Sherrington, a quiet and attractive village on the southern bank of the Wylye Valley. You proceed to the hamlet of Boyton with its handsome manor house and church and thence by lane to a crossing point. From here you climb a wooded track some 300 feet to Corton Hill, then turn left along a lane between fields and with wide views until Sherrington comes into sight once again when you descend to the village by field paths.

The main Salisbury-Warminster road runs along the Wylye Valley on the north side leaving the south side free of all traffic other than that serving local villages and farms. There is no pub in either Sherrington or Boyton — the nearest is the Carriers' Arms, a mile down the road at Stockton. There are some pleasant spots for a picnic though, particularly on the last leg of the walk before you descend the chalk escarpment above Sherrington.

If you start out from the church you might enjoy a brief diversion to a footbridge over the River Wylye: if so, turn left on leaving the church and then follow the track to the left towards the river. From the wooden footbridge you can gaze upon the shallow, wide, swiftly flowing and exceedingly clear waters of the River Wylye, a tributary of the Salisbury Avon renowned for its fishing. Notice, too, the thatched walls beside the track leading down to the river. There are not many surviving examples of thatched walls and this was the first example I had seen.

To begin the walk: with your back to the church turn right. At

61

the left bend you pass Rectory Cottage on the left – notice the Bible texts placed high on the end wall facing the lane. At this point walk along the track ahead towards the farm. Opposite the entrance to the farmyard bear left through a gate, into a field. Now turn right and follow the field boundary on the right hand side. Follow the edge of the field across two stiles until you reach the far right corner from which there is no exit. Here you should turn left and climb the edge of the field until you reach a gate on the right which leads you into the lane. Now turn right and follow the lane as it bears left, past some houses, then right before an entrance gateway to Boyton Manor. From here you can see the handsome, three gabled facade of the Manor House.

Next you pass the main entrance and driveway to the Manor. Here you must follow the lane until you reach the entrance drive to Boyton Church which, unfortunately, is generally kept locked, although it is surely worthwhile to approach the building in order to view its curiously arranged exterior. From the church entrance drive you continue to follow the lane, past a still flowing leat which, after following a course beside the lane, is abruptly diverted back to the Wylye.

At the crossing marked by a signpost indicating Upton Lovell to the right, turn left along a wooded track, including many large and spreading beech trees. Follow this track for a little over half a mile until you reach a group of agricultural buildings. Here you turn left to follow a metalled track past a pair of abandoned cottages. The cottages, which are evidently not very old, are built of flint in their lower courses, whilst the remainder of their walls are built of well squared blocks of hard chalk rock, or 'clunch', as it is known. Chalk rock and flint are the only parts of the great thickness of chalk strata which are of use as building stone.

Continue to follow the track — about a quarter of a mile past the abandoned cottages you reach the high point of the walk, around 580 feet. From the lane there is a view across the Wylye Valley towards the Codfords and the hills beyond. Follow the track past some woods and cattle sheds. About a quarter of a mile beyond the sheds a tumulus rises some 15 feet from the field to the left. Now you reach a fork which is not shown on the Ordnance Survey map. The metalled track continues to the right but you take the unmetalled track which forks left and begins to descend towards Sherrington. After a further quarter mile look out for an inconspicuous wooden stile in the fence on your left by which you leave the track to enter a field. Now head directly across this field towards a second stile in the fence opposite. From here you follow a somewhat sunken footpath to the right and down the face of the chalk escarpment.

At the bottom of the scarp bear right and follow the fence past two tumuli towards a gate beside a copse. Walk across the small field ahead towards a gate on the lane. Cross the lane and go through the gate opposite to cross a field surrounded by the buildings of Sherrington. Aim for the church on the north side of the village but, more immediately, for a stile on the opposite side. Now you cross the bridge built of railway sleepers across a stretch of water in the heart of the village which formerly comprised beds for the cultivation of watercress. Bear right at the lane, then turn left and right to reach the church again where the walk began.

The **Wylye Valley** was traversed by William Cobbett in 1826 and in his 'Rural Rides' he described it as follows: 'In coming from Salisbury, I came up the road which runs pretty nearly parallel with the river WYLY, which rises at Warminster and in the neighbourhood. This river runs down a valley twenty two miles long. It is not so pretty as the valley of the Avon; but it is very fine in its whole length from Salisbury to this place (Heytesbury). Here are watered meadows nearest to the river on both sides; then the gardens, the houses and the corn-fields. After the corn-fields come the downs; but, generally speaking, the downs are not so bold here as they are on the sides of the Avon.'

Cobbett observed an attractive, well ordered and productive landscape and yet he was dismayed and angered at the evident poverty of many who lived hereabouts: 'It is impossible for the eyes of man to be fixed on a finer country .... and it is not very easy for the eyes of man to discover labouring people more miserable.' He felt convinced that this land could sustain many more people, as indeed it once had. Cobbett blamed the parsons and their overseer-farmers who, he claimed, lived well off the labours of their subjects. On the other hand, Cobbett encountered unemployed workers from the cloth towns of Trowbridge and Bradford on Avon who were reduced to beggary and scavenging in the countryside. So perhaps it was the depression in industry as much as the changing conditions in the countryside which accounted for the widespread rural poverty.

Certainly, in Cobbett's time, the farming hereabouts was of the most modern and efficient kind. The water meadows were an example of this; the flat fields in the valley bottoms were kept moist by means of a complicated system of hatches and channels fed by the river. The running water helped to fertilise the ground by depositing silt, lessened the effects of late frosts and encouraged early growth; farmers were thus able to ensure more intense cultivation of their fields and to sustain a higher number of livestock per acre. As you walk along the lane past Boyton you will find a feeder channel beside the road diverted back to the river. In the field opposite, too, you can make out the gentle 'ridge and furrow' of the old water meadow, as water from the feeder channel was distributed over the entire field.

In Cobbett's day the downs almost solely comprised grazing for sheep: now the importance of sheep has sharply diminished. Thanks to modern fertilisers the downs, particularly those seen on this walk, are largely used to grow cereals and provide pasture for dairy farming.

Sherrington is a small but attractive village whose buildings are well spaced around the former watercress beds, fed by a spring which rises beneath the chalk hills just to the south. According to the Oxford Dictionary of English Place Names, the name 'Sherrington' is derived from the Old English 'scearn' meaning 'dung, filth, mud' — the village is referred to as 'Scarentone' in the Domesday Book. I had assumed that the 'Sher' part of 'Sherrington' was derived from the Old English 'Scir' meaning 'bright, pure' from which we get the common English place name of 'Sherborne', literally 'bright stream'. Should not the water from the spring which feeds the watercress beds, as well as the water of the Wylye, be described as bright and pure rather than as dung, filth and mud? It is very curious.

Sherrington Church is dedicated to Saints Cosmas and Damian, which is unusual. It is a small church which was rebuilt in the early seventeenth century and, apart from several windows which are from the earlier church and date from three centuries before, is pretty consistently of the Jacobean period. (An informative leaflet is obtainable inside the church). From the churchyard you can see the wooded eminence to the west on which a castle was built by the Giffords in Norman times, still partly surrounded by a moat fed by the Wylye.

Boyton has a small but handsome manor house of the early seventeenth century. The church of St Mary's has many interesting features, not least the curious configuration of its various constituent parts. It dates from the thirteenth century though it underwent extensive restoration in Victorian times.

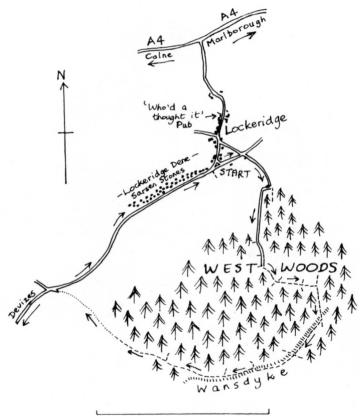

N

A4
Marlborough

A4
Calne

'Who'd a
thought it'
Pub

Lockeridge

Lockeridge Dene
Sarsen Stones

START

Devizes

WEST WOODS

Wansdyke

1 mile

West Woods
via Lockeridge and the Wansdyke

Distance: 4½ miles   **Time:** 2 hours

The walk is through quiet woodland and should appeal to anyone with a liking for such country, though it is perhaps advisable to choose a dry spell as the forest tracks can be heavy going in wet weather. The base for this walk is the village of Lockeridge which is situated in the Kennet valley about one mile south of the A4 and a few miles west of Marlborough. The minor road leading to Lockeridge is signposted on the A4, together with a sign indicating that there too may be found the pub curiously named the 'Who'd a Thought It'.

The route of the walk starts by a lane which leads from the village to West Woods, a sizeable but compact area of woodland set in an undulating landscape. Bridleways are followed through the woods, including one which runs beside a section of the Wansdyke. You emerge from the woods to a view across large open fields: the last mile of the walk is by a minor road to enter the village from the south via Lockeridge Dene, a small area of National Trust land.

There is no car park in Lockeridge but it is perhaps best to make for the southern end of the village. Space for your car can be found on the roadside towards the triangle of green opposite Lockeridge Dene. At this triangle the road forks — take the right fork which leads directly to Marlborough rather than to the A4 via Fyfield. Follow this road for a couple of hundred yards to bear right immediately past the house called 'High View'.

Follow the lane, rising gradually until you reach the woods. A notice tells you that this is Forestry Commission land known as West Woods and that the track straight ahead is a bridleway for the use of horse riders and walkers. Do not enter the wood here, however, but bear right and follow the lane by the edge of the wood. You will see that the woods here consist exclusively of tall beech trees growing closely together, each individual straining for the maximum light. Before you pass the farm on the right you should look behind to take in the view towards the Marlborough Downs on the north side of the Kennet valley, in particular to the rock strewn Fyfield Down. The rocks are sarsens composed of hard, compact sandstone and occur in quantity hereabouts. The farm buildings and houses further on are built of sandstone blocks.

Beyond the last house the track reaches a gate. Go through this gate and continue by the track through the woods. When you reach a cross track bear neither right nor left but carry on by the track opposite which ascends through the woods. As you ascend you will encounter some large sarsen stones beside the track and in the woods on either side. You can test these for hardness by scraping them with a coin or a key and find that this leaves no impression.

You reach first one crosstrack which you pass over to continue in the same direction, then a second crosstrack where the path levels out. This point is distinguished by a notice which reads 'Do not pick the daffodils please'. Here you turn right. You now follow this track for a couple of hundred yards until you reach a footpath, or minor track, leading away to the right, at an oblique angle. The route here is indicated by a pair of direction arrows on either side of the track. Bear right beside a large mound beside the track. This is the bank of the Wansdyke. The corresponding ditch is to the right; the footpath follows the bank on its left. If you miss the turning and reach a timber hide at a crosstrack you will know that you have gone too far and should retrace your steps until you pinpoint the Wansdyke path.

Now follow the the Wansdyke path; you can easily stray off into the wood if you do not keep sight of the bank of the dyke on your right. Eventually you reach a gate. On your right is a track which cuts right through the Wansdyke and this provides a good cross section of the ancient earthwork. The bank is certainly four feet high compared to the 'enemy territory' to the north.

Go through the gate to reach a track which runs parallel to the

Wansdyke and which follows the southern edge of West Woods. Turn right and follow the track with its views south across fields and north over the Wansdyke towards the woods. At a point marked by a line of trees forming a field boundary across the fields to the left, the track takes a double bend to change the 'inside', or bank side of the Wansdyke, for the 'outside', or ditch side. The track descends until you can see across a clearing on the right. At the bottom the track bends right, away from the Wansdyke. A grassy track lies straight ahead along the dip in the hills and heads back towards the gate where you entered the woods. The route entails bearing left here, to continue in the same general direction, by the track which now leads uphill.

When the track levels out you descend once again: at the bottom there is a long clearing on the right which once again leads back to the starting point in the woods. Carry straight on, uphill again and through a beech wood whose spreading branches form an almost continuous canopy of leaves. The Wansdyke has long since deserted us by heading across fields in a westerly direction towards Tan Hill.

As the path levels out you emerge from the woods and from this high point, around 732 feet, you have a wide view north and west. Straight ahead is a green track leading directly to the road which ascends the hill opposite to reach the village of East Kennett, out of view on the far side. To the right of the road is an unnamed hill which contains a single barn to the right of a track leading to West Overton, some very large fields, an occasional clump or line of trees and very little else. The uncluttered appearance, indeed bleakness, of this scene provides a striking contrast to the sights which have been crowding in on you during your walk through the woods: the spreading beeches, the sarsen stones and the tree stumps bedecked with luxuriant mosses, the bracken growing on the track edges, the wild flowers, the intimacy of the woodland environment.

Follow the track straight ahead to descend the field and reach the road. Bear right to follow the road for the remaining mile back to Lockeridge. First you encounter the signpost 'Lockeridge'. Then, on your left, is a National Trust sign indicating the sarsen strewn field on the left is Lockeridge Dene. The first house you see is built of red brick, not sandstone, but all the others past it are built of grey sarsen stone topped with thatch. A second National Trust sign gives some account of the sarsen stones.

Lockeridge is a puzzle. It is a village of moderate size containing many old houses as well as many more recent; there is a school, a shop and post office, a pub, a gospel hall, but neither chapel nor church. It is not one of those nineteenth century settlements full of artisans' houses which sprang up to serve some new, local industry and which the Church of England did not bother with. In Devon and Cornwall, such villages often have a Methodist chapel rather than a church. Lockeridge is even mentioned in the Domesday Book, so why is there no church?

Sarsen stones. The name is derived from 'saracen', or stranger, because these sandstone rocks bear no relation to the chalk strata on which they are found. They are also known as 'Grey Wethers', wethers being a name for sheep, because they appear in a field like grey sheep. Sarsens are found in many localities in southern England but it is on the Marlborough Downs where they are most numerous. Their origin is not completly clear, particularly as their original siting may have been affected by ice floes and by removal by man — prehistoric man built his monuments, like Avebury and Stonehenge, from sarsen stones. The sarsens in this locality most likely represent the residue of deposits, later than the chalk, which have been eroded until only the hard, resistant sandstone of the sarsens remain.

Wansdyke is a linear earthwork and occurs in two distinct parts, the east and west Wansdyke. The west Wansdyke runs in an east-west line south of Bath and Bristol whilst the east Wansdyke runs across the Marlborough Downs. The Wansdyke consists of a single bank with a ditch on the north side, thereby implying that it was built by a people living on the south side in defence against an enemy to the north. It is probable that it was built by the Britons, under the command of Ambrosius and his lieutenant Arthur, against the Saxons.